Skiing for Beginners

Skiing for

Beginners

A COMPLETE AND SIMPLE METHOD FOR CHILDREN AND THEIR PARENTS

by

CONRAD BROWN

Photographs by

NANCY GRAHAM

CHARLES SCRIBNER'S SONS, NEW YORK

CHARLES SCRIBNER'S SONS, LTD., LONDON

All of the sequence pictures in this book were made with
a 35 mm Bell and Howell Foton camera. Taking four to
six frames per second, it has a T2.2 Cooke amotal lens
and shutter speeds up to 1/1000 of a second.

ACKNOWLEDGMENTS

There is a good handful of friends to whom I am grateful for assistance on this book: Nancy Graham, for snapping the shutter at some two thousand "right times"; Cliff Taylor, for his counsel as a ski instructor and for his help as a supply packer on Mount Washington; to Messrs. Bell & Howell for the gracious loan of the Foton camera; to Joe Dodge's hutmen at the government shelter in Tuckerman's; but my deepest thanks go to Spike Mignault, who posed for all the pictures, and to whom every sequence of shots meant another rugged climb up the headwall of Tuckerman Ravine. My appreciation herewith to Spike's teacher and the Mad River Glen truant officer for letting me keep him out of school while we were taking pictures.

Conrad "Bruno" Brown

Mad River Glen
Vermont
March, 1950

CONTENTS

CONTENTS

Skiing for Beginners

FOREWORD TO THE PARENTS OF YOUNG SKIERS

Junior skiing has expanded rapidly in recent years. Across the country, in towns neighboring ski resorts, many school children receive free ski instruction in the wintertime. National Junior Championships are held annually. Educators have come to recognize the sport of skiing as a sound character builder. Skiing harnesses the natural "derring-do" that most children possess and directs it into the formation of such good qualities as courage, self-reliance, judgment and initiative.

SKIING FOR BEGINNERS is designed primarily to teach boys and girls in the nine-to-sixteen-year age group how to ski correctly. Most children younger than nine are really not ready for serious instruction, although the rule varies according to the child's temperament and physical development.

If you, as the parent of younger children, are a good skier, you can teach them to ski simply by letting them mimic you. Buy them skis about as long as they are tall and equip them the first year with Dartmouth children's ski bindings made of rubber. Then have your younger children follow you down a gentle grade and over a bump. They will soon learn to stand correctly over their skis by themselves, if you do *not* tell them to "bend your knees" but, instead, have them stand up straight. When they are used to skiing down and riding over a bump, have them follow you as you make a simple turn over a bump. By this easy method they will be making parallel christies in a surprisingly short time, with or without a bump to do them over. As they get older you may refer them to SKIING FOR BEGINNERS to help them understand the why and wherefore of their skiing.

Buy your children the best equipment you can afford for them to learn to ski on. They will progress much more rapidly with well-fitted ski boots and bindings on a good pair of steel-edged skis. They will be much safer, too, on good ski equipment. One final word to parents—don't worry—children hardly ever get hurt skiing.

TO THE YOUNG SKIER

Almost all of America's present skiing champions learned to ski when they were very young—perhaps nine or ten years old. If you are serious about learning to ski, it's a smart idea for you to learn good ski technique from the ground up—as early in life as you can. One of our aims in this book is to inspire you with the same spirit that has made experts of some of America's youngest skiers.

The Arlberg Technique is our choice for teaching you the fundamentals. With it you will learn to ski with confidence and style in the shortest possible time. Here is a standardized series of steps which allows for improvement all through your days of skiing. Some skiers may find that they can learn to "ski" in quite a short time by a helter-skelter method, but all too often they stop improving at a point far short of perfection. Many a discouraged poor skier has finally found that he has had to start all over from the beginning and learn the fundamentals to have any hope of becoming a really good skier.

Use this book as best you can by yourself, but do not neglect any chance to take lessons in an established ski school. The Arlberg Technique is so widely used that any good ski instructor can give you the same instruction that we give you here. You will find this book useful for ready reference before and after a day of skiing. Use it for review at the beginning of each season, for many skiers find that they must go back over the fundamentals when the first snow flies.

At every big ski resort these days one sees young skiers flashing down the slopes in perfect form, the envy of their elders who wish that they had been able to learn to ski when they were youngsters. Sometimes, however, the young skier forgets that control should come before speed. We admit that speed is truly the ultimate thrill in skiing, but the young skier should resist the temptation to "just let 'em ride" until he

TO THE YOUNG SKIER

has real mastery of his skis. Because accidents are usually the direct result of skiing out of control, technique and form should be the first concern of the beginner. We have all become familiar with the "basher" or "shussboomer". He is the inconsiderate fellow who tears straight down the slopes, with his skiis wide apart, arms and ski poles beating the air, wild-eyed with fright, yelling, "Track! Track!", and scaring everyone out of his way. It is he who is often responsible for the accidents which have made people call skiing one of the "dangerous sports". Unfortunately, it is some defenseless beginner carefully crossing the slopes who gets run down by the basher and suffers the broken bones. No one has to be a basher. This book teaches you how to ski safely, in control, with almost your first ride downhill.

In the practical suggestions that follow, I will first of all explain the whole maneuver as simply as possible. Then I'll let Spike take over with the pictures, explaining to you in his own words exactly what he is doing in each important part of each maneuver. When my explanation of a turn or position seems sufficient, Spike simply demonstrates, but wherever we feel his comments will help you, we have put them under the pictures.

Spike Mignault is a sturdy Vermonter. He is a real boy who loves the outdoors—particularly when it's snow-covered. Before Spike became the excellent young skier he is now, he took plenty of spills which we haven't got pictures of here. Both of us can tell you, though, that a real effort to ski well and correctly will bring you wonderful fun and thrills. It has brought them to us and many, many others.

But study closely the pictures of Spike. They tell you far more about correct positions of your body and skis than any long description in words can ever do. If you follow carefully the sequence of steps in SKIING FOR BEGINNERS and work hard to perfect your skiing, you will finally experience the supreme thrill of swinging away down a steep slope in a series of graceful controlled turns, whipping up behind you a sparkling plume of powder snow.

16

SKIS

The best low-priced skis are made of hard, close-grained hickory wood. The heavier and more expensive laminated skis are made of many pieces of wood glued together under tremendous pressure. Laminated skis are now definitely out of the experimental stage and are preferred by most skiers because they are much stronger than one-piece boards and do not warp so easily.

Have an expert pick out your skis for you. He will take into consideration your height and weight. The general rule is to get your skis about a foot longer than you are tall. Until you are eight or nine, however, you will not have had your skis much longer than your own height. No matter how short your skis are they will still seem too long for you when you get out on the slope for the first time. After a while you will realize the need for good long skis. They increase your stability as you increase your downhill speed. The camber is the bow or bend through the whole length of the ski and can be checked by placing the running surface on the floor. The space under the center should not be greater than one inch, and you should be able to press the two skis flat by standing evenly on both of them as they lie side by side.

After a ski of the correct length and stiffness has been chosen, your adviser will check to see that it is unwarped, straight-grained, and has a knot-free running surface with a straight groove down the center. There are several different kinds of skis for various types of skiing. The very narrow ash ski is used by the crosscountry racer and the long, wide, heavy, three-grooved model by the jumper. The so-called "downhill ski" is the best all-purpose model and is widely used by beginner and racer alike. It is a good idea to buy skis with clear bottom surfaces, since a coat of stain lacquer applied by the manufacturer may purposely hide defects. Steel edges for new skis are a *must*. You will be unable to ski in control on anything but new powder snow without these narrow strips of steel screwed to the outer edges of the running surfaces of your skis.

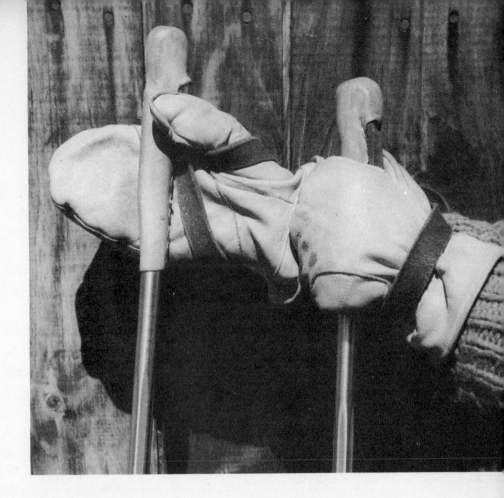

POLES

Do not try to ski without poles. They help you to keep your balance when skiing downhill and are necessary for climbing or walking on the level. The best ski poles are made with a steel shaft, though bamboo and laminated tonkin poles are also serviceable. When buying them, be sure that you get the proper length pole by turning them upside down and gripping them between the point and the ring. This will give you an idea of how long your poles will be when you are standing in the snow on your skis. While holding them this way in the store, your hand should come a little higher than your waistline when the handles of the poles are touching the floor. Out on the snow, to grip your poles correctly, slip your whole hand, thumb and all, up through the leather loop from below. The strap, rough side out, will pass over the back of your wrist. Your weight will then be supported by your straps when you are climbing or walking and you will be able to hold your poles more comfortably.

SKI BOOTS AND BINDINGS

Good ski boots are by far the most important part of your ski equipment. Your boots should have a roomy, square toe, a straight, sturdy sole, and a grooved heel. A good boot should have a steel shank running the length of the sole to stiffen the boot against the strong tension of a cable binding. You will want to wear two pairs of woolen socks, one medium weight and one heavy, when you ski. Be sure that you take ski socks with you when you try on new boots at the store. If you buy boots that are too tight you will be miserable on cold days because they will cut off your circulation; but boots that are too big will not give you good control of your skis. It really pays to take good care of your ski boots. Do not oil or grease them more than once a year, or the leather will become too pliable and your boots will stretch out of shape. During the ski season, the uppers ought to be polished every day with a good waterproof shoe polish. Ordinary ski lacquer should be painted along the seams and the sides of the soles to waterproof them as completely as possible. Never dry your boots before a fire or too near a hot radiator, and always keep boot trees in them when you are not using them. Remember to start the day with warm boots in cold weather and you will find your feet will not get cold so soon. It is important not to walk around in your boots any more than you have to, as walking bends the soles and stretches the leather.

No one can hope to ski properly without a good all-metal binding like the one in the picture. Do not have too much downward tension on your heels until you are making good christies; then you can unscrew the cable guides on the sides of your skis and move them back to within an inch of the heel springs. To be effective, the front throw clamp on your bindings should be hard to close. The toe irons should fit your boots snugly, with only half an inch, or less, of boot toe protruding through. If you plan to do any mountain skiing, you had better wear Arlberg straps attached to your cables and wound around your ankles to keep you from losing your skis in the case of a spill.

SKI CLOTHING

If you are a beginner you probably will dress too warmly the first time you go out skiing. Skiers have discovered over the years that if they wear tightly woven windproof clothing over several moderately thin layers of woolen clothing, they can be more comfortable even on the coldest days than if they wear heavy bulky clothes. There are definite style preferences which most skiers follow in the snow country.

First, the trousers should be of tightly woven fabric and the well-fitting "instructor" style. They should pull quite tightly from the waist to the ankles, but should be cut full enough in the knees to allow you to bend freely. Most skiers seem to prefer dark blue or black ski pants, but some favor the light neutral colors. In ski clothes, color makes little difference but dark colors stand out better against the snow and soil less easily. A windproof cotton poplin or nylon parka is well worth having. It should have a hood and should be long enough to tuck well down inside your trousers.

As for underclothing, long woolen underwear is not particularly necessary but it is certainly grand to wear when the temperature drops below zero and the north wind howls. You will ski better if you keep your legs good and warm. A cotton or flannel shirt and a tightly woven sweater should be worn under your parka. Sooner or later you may want a hand-knitted cable-stitch or Norwegian pattern ski sweater. The best ski caps have long ear flaps that protect the back of your neck as well as your ears, and tie under your chin. A bright cotton or silk scarf or bandana around your neck keeps the snow and wind from whipping down inside your shirt. The best ski mittens are the two-piece type leather "shells" over a pair of woolen mitts. Leather lasts longer on rope ski tows, too. Wear all your socks underneath your trousers. Why? Because the snow sticks to woolen socks worn on the outside, melts when you go indoors, and runs down inside your boots, making your feet damp. Then your feet are apt to freeze when you go outside again.

SKI WAXES

The art of ski waxing is quite complicated. Racers and old timers argue about it for hours on end. Until you become a really good skier, there are just a few simple facts you should know about waxing. At the beginning of each season, apply several base coats of some hard ski lacquer to give your boards a durable running surface and to protect the wood against dampness. After scraping all the old wax off and rubbing your skis down with cleaning fluid, put on the lacquer in thin, even coats with a one-inch paint brush. After each coat has thoroughly dried, rub it smooth with steel wool. If you want a base that will last and not chip or rub off too easily, five or six thin coats are better than two or three thick ones. Regular running waxes are applied over the lacquer to suit varying snow conditions. This wax should be put on freely and rubbed down with a warm iron or the palm of your hand. For top speed skiing, polish the wax with a cork but leave the surface bumpy.

There are hundreds of kinds of waxes and you can get all mixed up trying to find the right one. The simple rule of thumb is:

1. Hard wax for cold snow
2. Soft wax for wet sticky snow near freezing
3. Graphite paraffin for sticky new snow

The paraffin that is used for sealing jelly jars makes an ideal running surface for most skis. Carry a piece in your pocket and just scrub it on your skis if they seem to stick.

WALKING

Your first half hour on skis is likely to be a little jittery. RELAX— stay loose. Get used to the feeling of having your skis slipping under you by just walking around on them for a while. The main difference between ordinary walking and walking on skis is that you do not pick your feet up off the snow. Using your poles as if they were two canes, slide one ski forward and then the other. Jab your poles in and PUSH. Soon you will be able to walk along, keeping both skis sliding at once. See how smoothly you can learn to glide over the snow—and how fast you can go after a while. To turn on the level, just step around.

THE SIDE STEP

The side step is the most reliable climbing step.

Use it for going up and down very steep or difficult places. Side stepping is just like climbing stairs sideways. The left pole moves up with the left ski and the right pole with the right ski. But the best way to understand this maneuver is to look at these pictures of Spike and read his own explanation of what he is doing.

Keeping my knee bent, I pick up my uphill ski and place it one step higher.

Then I edge my uphill ski into the hill and step up onto it.

The lower ski joins the upper one and I repeat the process to keep climbing.

THE HALF SIDE STEP

The half side step is the easiest way to climb a gentle slope.

It is a combination of walking forward and side stepping. When you have made one long "zig" up across the slope, step around and "zag" up the other way—zig-zag all the way up.

27

THE HERRINGBONE

The herringbone is the fastest but most tiring way of climbing up.

Keep from crossing your skis in back by having your knees bent well forward into the hill. Make a wider "V" with your skis as the slope gets steeper. All you have to do is step from one ski over to the other, pushing with your poles at the same time.

THE KICK TURN

Stick your right pole in the snow ahead of you and your left pole by the tail end of your right ski. As if you were kicking a football, swing your left ski up and set its tail end in the snow. Next, let the ski drop away from you and set it down hard in the snow. The other ski can now be brought around easily. Notice how Spike uses his poles as props to help him keep his balance.

The kick turn is pretty tricky. If you want to, you can wait and practice it when you are more used to your skis. Or—you may just step around when you want to turn on a hill, keeping your poles stuck in the snow below you until you have gotten around.

ONE
PLANT POLES

TWO
KICK IT UP

THREE
OUT AROUND AND
SET IT DOWN

FOUR
OTHER SKI FOLLOWS

STRAIGHT DOWNHILL
RUNNING POSITION

Practice this at first on an easy hill with a long flat runout at the bottom. Stand up straight, completely relaxed in every muscle and joint. Skis should be the width of one ski apart—wider if it is icy. Keep your knees flexed a little forward to act as shock absorbers when you ski over bumps. Let your arms hang loosely. Your hands, held apart in front, should keep the poles pointed behind you. Tip forward enough to feel a pressure on your whole foot. Above all, *don't sit back.* Instead, stand right over your skis so that at all times you have the feeling that *you* are taking *them* down the hill. They should not take you for a ride. Of course, when the going gets steeper, you will have to tip a little farther forward from your ankles to stay over your skis.

THE SNOWPLOW POSITION

   The snowplow, correctly done, will give you your first real feeling of control. On an easy slope near the bottom of a hill, stick both poles in the snow downhill from you and step around into a wide snowplow position—points of your skis almost touching. Stand up straight, then kneel towards the front of your skis as far as you can without lifting your heels and you will be in correct snowplow position. Relax completely. Keep your tail in. Keep your skis evenly weighted and quite flat. Roll

your knees in together, after you are kneeling forward, just enough to make your skis gently brush across the snow as you move ahead. However, if the skis tend to cross in front, it means you are drawing your knees too close together. To flatten your skis just the right amount, pretend you are riding a big fat horse. As you are moving ahead, practice "putting on the brakes" by sinking abruptly and kicking your heels out wider at the same time. Then let the skis run together, pick up speed and put on the brakes again.

WHY BEND YOUR KNEES?

At some point in every skiing maneuver that you will learn from now on, you will be asked to "sink down" or "kneel forward" or "bend the knees from the ankles, please." Here's what happens when you press your knees forward properly without lifting up your heels: all the tendons in the back of your legs, from your heels to your hips, are pulled taut. This way you give yourself "automatic strength" without the slightest muscular effort. In fact, the more relaxed you are as you sink forward, the stronger your legs will be. An ankle at the end of a straight leg is wobbly, but you can't budge your ankle to either side at all when you have sunk your knees down forward. Try it!

THE SNOWPLOW TURN

When you decide you can do a fairly well controlled snowplow straight down the hill to a stop, try this experiment: Try putting more weight on one ski than the other as you snowplow down. You will find that you automatically turn slightly by weighting the ski that is pointed in the direction you wish to turn.

The snowplow turn is your most important basic maneuver because all fast skidded turns are just speeded up variations of the snowplow turn. Study Spike's pictures and explanations carefully. You will learn how to "wind up" for a turn. Winding up is done before every turn in skiing for the same reason that a baseball player draws his bat all the way back to his shoulder: To have some place to come *from* and swing *to*. You will learn how to drop your knee and your body straight down over your outside ski, without leaning out too far to the side as you make turns. Later you will sink your weight down equally onto *both* skis as they skid side by side through a wide, sweeping, fast christie.

Consider the snowplow and the snowplow turn as exercises—just steps on the road to good skiing. They are *not* to be done at anything but the slowest speeds. Don't let yourself become a "snowplow expert" and invite accidents. The snowplow position with the skis wide apart is dangerous to use if you are moving too fast. Please don't snowplow to stop if you *do* get going too fast—sit down and slide to a stop. The only really safe way to ski fast is with your skis side by side as much of the time as possible.

Here I am just finishing a snowplow turn to my left. I continue to sink down on my downhill (right) ski as long as I want to keep turning.

Now to windup for a turn to my right, I draw my left arm and shoulder back like this.

Then I flatten my skis a little to make them drift around until I am in the fall line (facing straight down the hill).

At this very important moment in the fall line, my outside (left) ski of the turn is pointing straight downhill. At this point I rotate my weight quickly over onto the outside (left) ski which makes me turn slowly to my right as I skid down the hill.

I sink my left knee, as deep as I can, down, down right straight towards the front of my ski so that I will continue to turn.

I try to keep my inside ski flat with very little weight on it. My body slowly, slowly rotates around, following the outside (left) ski as it turns. My right hand just comes back by my hip.

Now I have really finished the turn. To start another turn to my left, I wind up with my whole body, drawing my right arm and shoulder back this time. Notice that I lead with my left hand because I want to turn left. That's how to remember which way to wind up before making a turn.

TRAVERSING POSITION

To control your skis when you want to go across a slope you have to use a correct traversing position. Stand straight over your skis. Weight them both—a little more weight on the downhill ski. It's quite important to keep the uphill ski about half a boot-length ahead of the downhill ski. Let your knees flex forward just a little and relax completely. Practice traversing by skiing in this position all the way across a fairly steep slope—without skidding and without getting tense. At the other side, just step up the hill to stop. Better still, make a snowplow turn at the end of your traverse.

SIDESLIPPING FORWARD

To sideslip, moving slowly ahead across a steep slope, I just flatten my skis and tip a little bit forward with my knees bent.

SIDESLIPPING BACKWARD

To make my skis sideslip when I'm moving slowly backward, I just let my weight go a little back on my heels.

SIDESLIPPING

Straight sideslipping is hard to do unless you can find a smoothly packed and quite steep slope. With your legs, boots and skis locked tightly together, just let your ankles bow out from the hill enough to flatten your skis, and you will begin to sideslip. Push against the hill with your upper ski pole if you want to. Practice this for a while to get the feeling of having your skis skidding under you, because you must realize that every turn in skiing from here on is a controlled sideslip.

WIND UP

I draw my downhill (right) arm back and twist my whole body around facing downhill to wind up like this. Then I start across the hill, riding on both skis.

ROTATE AND SINK DOWN

I rotate and sink down onto the downhill ski to make both skis skid.

FOLLOW THROUGH

To make my skis continue skidding and turning, I tip forward in this position, leaning a little into the hill, until I stop sideslipping.

SIDESLIPPING BY TURNING UP
INTO THE HILL

This is an easier way to practice sideslipping. Pick a good steep, well-packed place to practice this maneuver. Wind up with your whole body before you start to move across the hill. Remember, it's your *downhill* shoulder and arm that you wind up. You should sink down fast onto your lower ski to release the grip of the snow on your skis and make them start skidding. Rotate your body around slowly as you sideslip from one place on the hill to another five or ten feet farther down the slope. Wind up, sideslip, let the skis run, wind up, sideslip again—two or three times as you cross the practice slope.

A RULE

This rule applies to all your skiing: Whenever you make your skis start to skid, sink your knees down forward to control the skid. Straight legs and flopping ankles never controlled a skidding ski!

I can make my skis turn easily and drop suddenly to skid down the front side of the bump. They drop fast but I drop faster to keep up with them as they skid.

This is how I turn right on top of a bump. Notice that my skis are off the snow in front and in back. I am winding up to make a turn down to my left.

46

TURNING OVER A BUMP

If you find a nice little bump, don't ski around it every time. Try making a simple turn over the bump—it's fun and very easy. See how only the middle of Spike's skis touch the snow when he's right on top. That's the exact moment to rotate and sink down over the other side of the bump, facing in your new direction. Make your skis skid, side by side and close together, if you can.

Sometimes I don't feel like turning, so I just crouch way down and JUMP up when my skis get right on top of the bump. Jumping helps my sense of balance—and besides, it's lots of fun to see how far you can go!

WIND UP

I start down the fall line in a fast, wide, flat-ski snowplow. Here I draw my right arm and shoulder back.

ROTATE TO OUTSIDE SKI

When I've got some speed up, I rotate my weight onto the downhill (right) ski which is pointed in the direction I want to turn to (my left) and . . .

SKIS TOGETHER AND SINK DOWN

. . . immediately slide the other (left) ski in and shove it slightly ahead. As soon as the skis are together, I sink down in my knees to control their skidding.

ROTATE THROUGH AS THE SKIS SKID

By banking into the turn a little, all I have to do now is ride around the sweep of the turn on my skidding skis. My body rotates slowly around through the whole snowplow christie.

SNOWPLOW CHRISTIE DOWN THE FALL LINE

Now you are ready to combine your snowplow turns with your side-slipping to do a snowplow christie. This should be very easy for you. Just think of it as an ordinary snowplow turn "with all the motions speeded up" and a skid on the end of it. Don't sit back when you rotate to turn, but rather rotate somewhat forward onto the outside ski. Sink your knees down to skid and turn at the same time. Try banking *into* your turn as the skis skid and see how much easier it is. Imagine you are an airplane banking around a turn.

By tipping forward a little, I make my skis start to turn into the fall line.

When my outside (right) ski points straight down, I rotate my weight onto it.

Then I slide the inside (left) ski in to bring the skis together.

I lean in as they skid.

As I continue to turn, my whole body follows through.

Crossing the slope in snowplow position, I wind up.

SNOWPLOW CHRISTIE
ACROSS THE FALL LINE

When you can make pretty good snowplow christies from a straight snowplow down the fall line, try one like this. You'll need a little more speed. Be sure you practice these turns on a fairly steep slope. It is easier to turn when the force of gravity helps the tails of your skis to drop down and around into a skid.

Notice the bend in my ankles as I sink down in my knees throughout the turn.

51

THE WINDUP POSITION

Whether it is done fast or slow, in a tight or a wide sweeping arc, any christie can be done more easily if you prepare for it properly when you wind up. Study this picture. This is the "reverse twist" position you should always drop into WITH YOUR WHOLE BODY before you try to do a stem christie.

As you cross the slope in correct traversing position, simply step forward and down onto the lower ski in a half snowplow. It's like snowplowing with only one ski instead of both. Don't use this position to check your speed, but only to put you in a good windup for the turn. At the same moment that you step down and forward onto your downhill ski, draw the opposite (uphill) arm and shoulder back. Make sure your downhill shoulder, too, is pressed well forward before you rotate into your turn.

It is very important always to drop down into deeply bent knees in this windup position. Practice this on the side of a hill while you are standing still until it seems like second nature to drop onto the downhill ski and wind up before *every* turn.

THE STEM CHRISTIE

The stem christie is a fairly high speed turn. As you gain confidence enough to begin skiing faster, you will use variations of the stem christie for all your turns. If you possibly can, find a big, wide open slope to learn these on. The idea is to see how long you can continue turning and turning and at the same time skidding and skidding throughout as wide an arc as the terrain will allow. When you are on a fast, narrow trail, the arc of your stem christies will have to be small, of course. But even then don't EVER pick a spot ahead of you and try to turn on it. The faster you ski, the more you will try to make your turns close to the fall line. Traverse less. Make all the motions of your windup and rotation much more flowing and smooth. You will need to open your skis much less when you wind up. Rotate your weight very slowly throughout the turn. Try to keep your skis close together. Though you won't have to sink your knees down much, you will still have to be quick to sink them the instant you start your rotation and your skis begin to skid and turn.

as I follow through . . .

to finish the stem christie.

I wind up . . .

Rotating my weight onto the outside (left) ski, I quickly slide the other (right) ski in beside it and bank into the turn.

The skis are side by side by the time I reach the fall line.

From here on—my skis skid to the outside as I turn.

I sink down to keep my skis from sliding out from under me . . .

d make them bite . . .

See how soon before your outside ski points down the fall line you can "pull the prop out." The "prop" is your leg over the inside ski. In other words, with correct windup and enough speed, you should be able to rotate your weight to your outside ski and quickly slide the inside ski over beside it. Then just ride out the whole long exciting skid of the turn with both skis side by side. It's like having two outside skis in your turn if you can get them close enough together. Pull the prop out, slide 'em together, sink a little, lean in a bit—and then see how long you can keep them skidding.

BANKING AROUND A TURN

As you begin to ski faster you will find that you must sway over or bank into your turns. It is very important to be conscious of doing this all the time. Banking will make your skis bite into the snow and will help you turn in the direction you want to go. Think of the way you bank with your WHOLE BODY on your bicycle when you go around a curve. Make fast turns—and sharp turns—the same way on skis.

WIND UP . . .

AND . . .

BANK OVER . . .

INTO THE TURN . .

HIGH SPEED TURN

Try making fast smooth christies, barely opening your skis. Just wind up, rise a little and bank over into the turn. Then wind up and bank over the other way as you slowly rotate through a series of wide flowing turns. As soon as you are able to ski fast, try to "cut" long sweeping arcs in your turns, holding your skidding to a minimum.

AND . . .

FOLLOW THROUGH

59

SKATING ON SKIS

Skating on skis is very similar to skating on skates. Just step off on an angle to the left on the left ski. Then step off on an angle to the right on the right ski. It's great fun to practice skating and it is well to be good at it if you ever expect to do any racing.

After you have learned to skate, try a trick
turn like this. It's called a "royal."

Competitive Skiing: Running a hairpin in a slalom course.